Little Monster's
Mother Goose

D1123261

for Len,
the best Little Monster from Georgia

Little Monster's Mother Goose

by
Mercer Mayer

Golden Press • New York

Western Publishing Company, Inc.
Racine, Wisconsin

Copyright © 1979 by Mercer Mayer. All rights reserved.
No part of this book may be reproduced or copied in any form without written
permission from the publisher. Printed in the U.S.A.
Golden®, A Golden Book®, and Golden Press® are trademarks of
Western Publishing Company, Inc.

Library of Congress Catalog Card Number: 78-78243
ISBN 0-307-13742-2

LEANING TOWER
PROPERTY OF ISLAND JOE LTD.

Donkey, donkey, old and gray,
Open your mouth and gently bray;
Lift your ears and blow your horn,
To wake the world this sleepy morn.

If I had a donkey that wouldn't go,
Would I beat him? Oh, no, no.
I'd put him in the barn and give him some corn,
The best little donkey that ever was born.

Dingty, diddlety,
My mammy's maid;
She stole oranges,
I'm afraid.
Some in her pocket,
Some in her sleeve;
She stole oranges,
I do believe.

The cock's in the woodpile
Blowing his horn;
The bull's in the barn
A-threshing the corn.
The maid's in the meadow
A-making the hay;
The Croonies in the river
Are swimming away.

Margaret wrote a letter,
Sealed it with her finger,
Threw it in the dam
For the dusty miller.
Dusty was his coat,
Dusty was the silver,
Dusty was the kiss
I'd from the dusty miller.
If I had my pockets
Full of gold and silver,
I would give it all
To my dusty miller.

Little girl, little girl,
Where have you been?
I've been to see Grandmother
Over the green.
What did she give you?
Milk in a can.
What did you say for it?
"Thank you, Grandam."

Hie to the market, Jenny come trot,
Spilt all her buttermilk, every drop.
Every drop and every dram,
Jenny came home with an empty can.

Hearts, like doors, will open with ease
To very, very little keys;
And don't forget that two of these
Are "I thank you" and "If you please."

When I was a little boy
I had but little wit;
'Tis a long time ago,
And I have no more yet;
Nor ever, ever shall,
Until I die,
For the longer I live
The more fool am I.

Leg over leg,
As the Kerploppus went to Dover,
When he came to a pail,
Jump he went over.

Rain on the green grass,
And rain on the tree,
Rain on the house-top,
But not on me.

Evening red and morning gray,
Send the traveller on his way;
Evening gray and morning red,
Bring the rain upon his head.

Every fiddler, he had a fine fiddle,
And a very fine fiddle had he;
Twee, tweedle-dee, tweedle-dee, went the fiddlers.
Oh, there's none so rare as can compare
With King Cole and his fiddlers three.

Cobbler, cobbler, mend my shoe,
Get it done by half past two;
Stitch it up and stitch it down,
Then I'll give you half a crown.

Matthew, Mark, Luke, and John,
Hold this donkey till I leap on.
Hold him steady, hold him sure,
And I'll get over the misty moor.

Little Monster, fellow fine,
Can you shoe this horse of mine?
Yes, good sir, that I can,
As well as any other man.
There's a nail and there's a prod,
And now, good sir, your horse is shod.

Jenny, come tie my,
Jenny, come tie my,
Jenny, come tie my bonny cravat.
I've tied it behind,
I've tied it before,
I've tied it so often, I'll tie it no more.

If I'd as much money as I could spend,
I never would cry, "Old chairs to mend!
Old chairs to mend! Old chairs to mend!"
I never would cry, "Old chairs to mend!"

If I'd as much money as I could tell,
I never would cry, "Old clothes to sell!
Old clothes to sell! Old clothes to sell!"
I never would cry, "Old clothes to sell!"

There was a little boy went into a barn,
And lay down on some hay;
An owl came out and flew about,
And the little boy ran away.

Hark! Hark! The dogs do bark,
Beggars are coming to town;
Some in rags and some in tags,
And some in velvet gowns.

Christmas is coming,
The geese are getting fat;
Please to put a penny
In the old dragon's hat.
If you haven't got a penny,
A ha'penny will do;
If you haven't got a ha'penny,
Then God bless you!

Moll-in-the-Wad and I fell out,
And what do you think it was all about?
I gave her a shilling, she swore it was bad,
"It's an old soldier's button," said Moll-in-the-Wad.

Naughty paughty Jack-a-Dandy
Stole a piece of sugar candy
From the grocer's shoppy-shop,
And away did hoppy-hop.

There was an old woman lived under the hill,
And if she's not gone she lives there still.
Baked apples she sold, and cranberry pies,
And she's the old woman that never told lies.

One thing at a time
And that done well,
Is a very good rule,
As many can tell.

Hickory, dickory, dock,
There's a Croonie on the clock.
The clock struck three,
The Croonie did flee,
Hickory, dickory, dee.

Sing a song of sixpence,
A pocket full of rye;
Four-and-twenty black bats
Baked in a pie.

The King was in the countinghouse,
Counting out his money;
The Queen was in the parlor,
Eating bread and honey;
The maid was in the garden,
Hanging out the clothes;
When down came a Bombanat
And snipped off her nose.

Rub-a-dub-dub,
Three men in a tub;
And who do you think they be?
The butcher, the baker,
The candlestick-maker;
Turn 'em out, knaves all three!

Wee Willie Winkie runs through the town,
Upstairs and downstairs, in his nightgown;
Rapping at the window, crying through the lock,
"Are the children all in bed, for now it's eight o'clock."